AFFIRM
S

How to live the life of your dreams through positive thinking

By Sue Searle BSc, PGDip, RGN

"The quality of your thoughts determines the quality of your life."
Vera Peiffer

Second Edition
2012

*To Conor
Best wishes
Sue :)*

> *"By your thoughts you are daily, even hourly, building your life; you are carving your destiny."*
> Ruth Barrick Golden

This little book aims to guide you through the use of Affirmations to empower you and help you reach the success you deserve. Affirmations are powerful self-talk that will help you think more positively. You will start to change your mindset to one that will empower you, give you confidence, and help you to move forward to live the life of your dreams! It will help in all areas of your life such as love, relationships, losing/gaining weight, health, happiness, and career.

About the Author

Sue Searle has a degree in Biological Sciences and is a trained nurse with 15 years experience. She runs several businesses including a coaching business, a travel company, an ecological consultancy and a property business. She lives in the south-west of England and has two grown-up children. She loves travelling, art, photography, coaching and business.

To find out more about her coaching programs see:

www.thelifeyouchoose.net

Message from the Author:

I have always been a naturally 'positive', 'can do' person but it wasn't until recent years that I realized that actually there were many negative thoughts also going through my mind. These doubts, limiting beliefs and fears were holding me back and I hadn't even realized.

I started working with a coach, Anthony McGloin, in 2006, who opened my eyes to the possibilities beyond this state of mind and the life I was living through his coaching and guided reading.

It took a lot of practice and vigilance to work through fears, beliefs and negative thought habits that I had developed. Many of which I had acquired very early in my life and they were certainly not serving me now.

I am now a happy, healthy, wealthy, loving, calm and peaceful person who lives a rich life of endless possibility. Good things happen in my life all the time, I attract wonderful people and I (usually) only see the good side of this wonderful world of ours.

I have written this book in order to help others to benefit from what I have learnt. I hope you find it useful on your journey to the life of your dreams.

Legal Disclaimers & Notices

All rights reserved. No part of this book may be reproduced or transmitted in any form, electronic or otherwise, by any means without the prior written permission of the publisher.

This book is presented to you for informational purposes only and is not a substitution for any professional advice. The contents herein are based on the views and opinions of the author and all associated contributors.

While every effort has been made by the author and all associated contributors to present accurate and up to date information within this document, it is apparent that technologies and philosophies rapidly change. Therefore, the author and all associated contributors reserve the right to update the contents and information provided herein as these changes progress. The author and/or all associated contributors take no responsibility for any errors or omissions if such discrepancies exist within this document.

The author and all other contributors accept no responsibility for any consequential actions taken, whether monetary, legal, or otherwise, by any and all readers of the materials provided. It is the reader's sole responsibility to seek professional advice before taking any action on their part.

Readers results will vary based on their skill level and individual perception of the contents herein, and thus no guarantees, monetarily or otherwise, can be made accurately. Therefore, no guarantees are made.

Contents

Legal Disclaimers & Notices	5
Contents	6
1. Introduction	7
2. Why Make An Affirmation?	101
3. How To Make Affirmations	32
4. Useful Affirmations	42
5. Cosmic Affirmations	46
6. The Chemistry of Affirmations	501
7. Affirmations for everyday use	55

Chapter 1
Introduction

"All that we are is the result of what we have thought. The mind is everything.

What we think we become."
The Buddha

The Concise Oxford Dictionary states:
ăffir'm – *assert strongly, state as fact, confirm, ratify, make formal declaration.*
ăffirmā'tion- affirming, solemn declaration. The Collins English Dictionary defines affirmation as: "A statement of the truth of something; assertion."

Affirmations are a powerful ingredient in positive thinking. They are not statements that you *wish* to be true; they are statements that you believe *are* true.

Affirmations are positive statements describing a desired condition in your life. That condition may not yet exist, but the affirmation is spoken as though it does. A simple example might be: "I am at peace with my life." This is repeated several times on a daily basis, out loud or mentally, the aim being to program the subconscious mind into producing the desired outcome. Affirmations must be sincerely felt, and spoken in the present tense with conviction and enthusiasm.

We carry out such mental programming every day whether we know it or not; the trick is to make this programming *conscious* and *positive*. The alternative is to be unaware that we are issuing negative affirmations to ourselves. If you have ever made a mistake and muttered "I am such an idiot", you have given yourself a negative affirmation. The problem is that any negative affirmation you give enters your subconscious mind and has a harmful effect – it creates your reality.

Positive thinking as a popular psychology can be traced back to 1937, with Napoleon Hill's bestselling book *Think and Grow Rich*. Mr Hill studied highly successful people for 30 years and wrote this book to summarise his findings on what made these people so successful. He also outlines many techniques that he used to create his own amazing and empowering reality. This book remains important today, although there have been countless similar guides written since on the subject of positive thinking for personal success since then.

Many books on positive thinking, like *Think and Grow Rich*, focus mainly on the financial benefits to be gained from altering your thoughts. The reason for this is obvious: it taps into the desire of so many people to become wealthy. Wealth is also measurable. Whilst books on creating wealth may be geared to capturing the public imagination, it may also give doubters and newcomers the wrong impression. People buy these books expecting some incredible revelation, and do not expect to be told that all they have to do is start thinking positively.

The answer is so simple it is easy to dismiss it, but simple does not always mean easy. Reprogramming a mind that has suffered negative thoughts and affirmations for years can be tough. We experience 60,000 thoughts a day and for some up to 40,000 are negative! No wonder some of us struggle to feel positive.

The good news is that you can reprogram your thoughts, with a little vigilance and through affirmations, to virtually eliminate negative thoughts. What would you do if you were not afraid? What would your life be like if you had virtually no negative thoughts? I suspect you would feel empowered, confident, and happy and you would get a lot more done! In fact your life would be totally different.

Despite the plethora of *Think and Grow Rich*-type books, positive thinking is infinitely more than trying to make yourself rich. The people most likely to get rich off such financially-oriented books on positive thinking are probably the authors. The rest of us can be left feeling a little cheated, and therefore disillusioned with the whole notion.

Having said that, it is important to read these books and gain new ideas, insights and inspiration and to hear success stories. If your mind thinks something is possible then you are almost there in terms of achieving that thing.

Positive thinking has the power to transform your life, in all areas, and affirmations are the cornerstone of beginning and maintaining this successful transformation. You of course have to take action too!

"One comes to believe whatever one repeats to oneself sufficiently often, whether the statement be true or false."

Robert Collier

Chapter 2
Why Make An Affirmation?

"An affirmation is a statement of fact, or what you intend to be fact, and you make it over and over again."
David R Hamilton

Personal Goals

Positive affirmations are made because you want to achieve something. That may be more money, a new car, a bigger house, a better job, more success, or, on a more personal level, love, health, happiness or inner peace. We all have such desires – we would be strange if we didn't. But these outcomes can sometimes seem so far beyond our grasp that we do not really dare to think that they could be ours for the asking. Instead, we focus on how far away from our desired outcomes we are and negative affirmations become our mantra.

- We desire to be wealthy, so we think: *I'm never going to be rich.*
- We want that promotion, so we think: *It's bound to go to someone else.*
- We want love in our life, so we think: *No one's going to love me.*

We *are* thinking about the things we want, but from a *negative* perspective. If this is true, then there should be no doubt as to why it is a good idea to flip the coin and start talking positively. It is not as though we are being forced to start doing something we aren't doing already, or that is in any way laborious. How much effort does it take to say one sentence to yourself? And wouldn't it be nice to speak to yourself in positive terms for a change?

Case study:

I was speaking to a 40 year old man recently who said he was a 'slow learner'. He then proceeded to tell me that he was debt free (paid off his mortgage), had a good job and was enjoying learning about wealth creation in our workshop. I pointed out that calling himself a 'slow learner' was a negative affirmation and if he has kept on saying that to himself over the years then by now he must believe it - deeply. We then discussed the matter further and what he actually meant was that he found it difficult to learn by reading and found himself reading something over and over again before he 'got it'. I said, 'If you *listened* to it or *did* it would you learn quickly?' 'Yes,' he said. I told him about the different styles of learning and pointed out that he probably just wasn't the type to learn by reading (visual). If he used 'doing' (kinaesthetic) or 'hearing' (auditory) methods of learning he would probably be fine.

I suggested that instead of buying books he buy audio books and listen to them in the car on the way into work. I then suggested that he come up with another affirmation about himself – such as

'I learn quickly and easily' or *'I love learning and I find it easy.'*

Be Careful What You Wish For

You will doubtless have heard this saying in the past. In full, it says: "Be careful what you wish for; you may just get it."

This may appear an odd saying, because who in their right mind would wish for negative things to happen? Unfortunately, most of us are thinking negative thoughts every day. Look at the examples on page 11 – how easy it is to have a positive desire that is expressed in a negative way?

Take the example of your desire for a promotion. Instead of repeating to yourself: "The promotion is mine", you think: *It's bound to go to someone else.* Perhaps this is a means of protecting yourself from disappointment, but what you are actually doing is repeating a negative affirmation.

Your subconscious is receiving the message that you will not be promoted, and it interprets this as an 'order'. You may think that your subconscious cannot affect the decision made by your boss, but your negativity comes through loud and clear. Your boss may be looking at you and feel reluctant to promote you because they sense you are not the positive person they want in a position of increased power, or you don't really want it..

So you fail to win the promotion largely because you have been thinking you won't, and your boss has picked up on something negative that they don't like. Although you didn't actually *wish* that you would fail, you helped make it happen because failure was the dominant thought in your mind.

The saying "Be careful what you wish for, you may just get it" may speak of wishes, but it more correctly refers to thoughts that are uppermost in your mind for the majority of the time. In other words: "Be careful what you *think of*; you may just get it."

The results that are manifested in your life can be directly affected by the thoughts in your head and the affirmations you give to yourself. If you really think about it, could this be true of you? Have your *thoughts* affected your *results*?

Have you heard the tragic story of Midas? He wished that everything he touched would turn to gold. This was great, and indeed everything he touched did turn to gold. His wealth grew with every touch. Unfortunately, however, this wish was taken literally and as his child ran up to him and she gave him a hug, she turned to gold. A solid gold statue, extremely valuable but was it as precious as his child? The same happened to his wife. She too turned to solid gold, but was she as precious now? So you can see from this mythical example that you have to be very specific about what you wish for.

The PMA/NMA Coin

Another good reason to create positive affirmations for yourself is because it is so simple to do. As already mentioned, that does not mean it is necessarily an *easy* process to carry out – we will deal with this in the next chapter (remember your 40,000 negative thoughts?) – but it is certainly a simple process to *understand*.

In positive thinking, your mental attitude is often referred to as a coin. It is an apt description. You have two forms of mental attitude: a Positive Mental Attitude (PMA), and a Negative Mental Attitude (NMA). Just like the heads and tails of a coin. And just like a coin, it can be flipped very easily and it will never come to rest on its edge. This means there is no third option of a neutral mental attitude. It is either *positive* or it is *negative*.

When something is so easy to understand, there is very little reason to simply stare at your coin and leave it lying there with its NMA side upwards. Whenever you notice that you are feeling negative, or you catch yourself making a negative comment to yourself, make a conscious effort to flip the coin to its PMA side, and counter the negative thought with a positive affirmation.

As wonderfully complex as your mind is, it does not have the capability to focus on more than one thought at any one time. If you are thinking a negative thought, you can instantly dismiss it by bringing a positive thought to mind. It sounds easy to say it like that, and it can be. But it takes practice and vigilance.

Louise L Hay, in her book 'You Can Heal Your Life' explores the concept of 'what you put your attention to, grows'. She gives the following list of examples of poor affirmations (or unintentional self-talk):

I don't want to be fat
I don't want to be broke
I don't want to be old
I don't want to live here
I don't want to have this relationship
I don't want to be like my mother/father
I don't want to be stuck in this job
I don't want to have this hair/nose/body
I don't want to be lonely
I don't want to be unhappy
I don't want to be sick

By fighting a negative with a negative you will never gain a positive – it just doesn't work like that! We constantly hear the press and governments saying they are 'fighting terrorism', 'battle against cancer', 'winning the war against …'.

You cannot change to a positive with a negative. So going back to the above statements these are the alternative, positive versions that will create a positive outcome:

I am slender
I am prosperous

I am eternally young
I now move to a better place
I have a wonderful (new) relationship
I am my own person
I love my hair/nose/body
I am filled with love and affection
I am joyous and happy and free
I am totally healthy

Note these are worded in the *present* and contain *positive* words to focus on.

Tip
If you are having a lot of negative thoughts, try this (devised by Mark Victor Hansen):

Get a thick rubber band and put it around your wrist. Every time you catch yourself having a negative thought or doing negative self-talk grab the elastic band and snap it against your wrist. It will hurt a bit and if you are having a lot of them your wrist might get quite sore! The idea is to practice *noticing* your negative thoughts and start to re-programme yourself to change them into positive thoughts. Eventually your wrist won't hurt any more!

Loving Yourself

One pinch point for changing to a positive mental attitude is your own self-image. Can you look in the mirror, stare into your own eyes and say 'I love you'? Probably not – for some people this is *very* difficult if not impossible. It is essential that you concentrate on increasing your self image. You can be your worst enemy with self-talk that destroys all your efforts to move forward. Rather, you need to be your own *best friend* and to love yourself.

Start by saying to yourself over and over again 'I approve of myself'. By saying this you may get some negative self-talk emerging. Statements like 'Who do you think you are?', 'What do you think you are doing?', 'You're an idiot!' may come up. The good news is this is the first stage towards ridding yourself of negative self-talk. If you first recognise these negative words of disapproval, self-loathing or self-criticism you can start to work on ridding yourself of them. Whenever anything comes up say 'I approve of myself exactly as I am.' Gently say to the negative thoughts 'I let you go.'

With consistent effort on recognising negative self-talk, and letting it go, you will eventually rid yourself of it completely. This might seem impossible at first, but I can assure you it *is* possible and only having positive thoughts and loving yourself is a *very* nice place to be!

You may find it helpful to write down the negative thoughts and the positive affirmation that will replace it. As you replace the negative with the positive you will become happier, at peace with yourself and find new inner confidence. You will become your own best friend. This is an enormously empowering exercise and feeling good about yourself is the basis for moving forward with your life.

Go With Gratitude

To help you become more positive you should also practice *gratitude*. What I mean by that is to recognise what is *good* in your life now and *be grateful* for it. Every morning, when you wake, greet the day with a list of things you are grateful for.

Examples include:

I am so happy and grateful that I am alive
I am so happy and grateful that I am loved
I am so happy and grateful that the sun is shining
I am so happy and grateful that I have a great job/home/family/partner/pet etc

Come up with your own list. It may be different every day or you may have the same core ones and add a few other things each day as appropriate. Stand or sit up straight and hold your head up and say it with enthusiasm and with a smile on your face!

Use this exercise to notice the things that we take for granted like the sun, food on your plate, your home, job, partner, children or colleagues. Your list can be as long as you like! In fact the longer it is the better! It certainly makes you think.

When I work with people who are in a negative state they find this quite difficult, so start with some obvious ones like – I am alive, the sun is shining etc. Avoid negative versions like 'I am so happy and grateful I am not dead', rather use 'I am so happy and grateful to be alive!', or 'I am so happy and grateful it is not raining', rather use 'I am so happy and grateful that the sun is shining (or) it is a beautiful/dry day'. Rid your vocabulary of negative words where possible.

By being grateful for the things around you, you can start to recognise that there is a lot of good around you and just by noticing these things it will help you to focus on good things rather than bad or negative things.

Controlling and Understanding the Subconscious Mind

Your conscious mind is like the tip of an iceberg. The subconscious mind is the vast hidden part of the iceberg which lies beneath the surface, unseen. The power of your subconscious should not be underestimated, and what it contains may not be known by you until you start to work on ridding it of negative thoughts, ideas and beliefs.

These thoughts, ideas and beliefs have been filtering into your mind since you were born through your parents, family, teachers, employers, the media and your friends. You see the world, as you understand it, through the filter of these thoughts, ideas and beliefs. They are unique to you and you might have noticed that in any given situation, you will react to or interpret the situation very differently to anyone else.

Controlling and understanding your subconscious mind is a useful life-skill, and affirmations can help forge closer links between your conscious mind and your subconscious mind.

Once you start making your positive affirmations and you begin to see that they are working, you have proven your ability to control a part of yourself that remains out of reach to so many other people. Your subconscious mind is like the registry of your computer. A computer's registry is its database that stores configuration settings and options. Most people have a vague idea it's there, some may realize what it does, but very few will be able to open it up and start deleting or adjusting any of its keys or values because they won't know what anything in there means.

You need to understand that it is possible to adjust your subconscious mind, and positive affirmations are one powerful way to do this. It is how you can clear out all the redundant and harmful data your subconscious stores, and allow you to know exactly why you may be behaving in a certain way in a certain situation. When a computer is behaving oddly or sluggishly, it is often a muddled and messed up registry that's responsible. Even when you delete a program, there will usually be remnants of it remaining in the registry. Your aim with positive affirmations is to reprogram your subconscious, and to continue to clear out any negative traces that remain from your previous way of thinking.

Positive affirmations help you become more in tune with how your subconscious operates, and why you may respond poorly in certain circumstances. The more you program your mind positively, the more easily you will recognize negative activity and be able to jump on it and delete it. Equally, you will find that you are far more tuned into the whisperings of your subconscious mind that often brings answers to difficult dilemmas in your life.

Overcoming Bad Habits

Depending on how they are phrased, affirmations can create good or bad habits. You may start out with affirmations that relate to some grand goals, such as a better career, being a millionaire, or having a more peaceful or loving life, but don't forget that affirmations can be applied to any area of your life. They can be used to help control your weight, to quit smoking, to cut back on the booze, or to stop biting your fingernails. You name the habit, and a positive affirmation can be phrased to deal with it. For this reason it is a good idea to make your own bespoke affirmations to deal with your own particular dreams or issues.

Case Study 1:

Linda was overweight. She had tried every diet in the book over a number of years and she was becoming despondent about the lack of results.

Diets seemed to work for a while then she would slip back to her larger self again. We first started to work on Linda's self-image as she lacked confidence. Affirmations included 'I am a happy healthy person, I love life, everything is going perfectly, I am loved and love others, I approve of myself. I love myself.'

At first she felt silly saying those things and when she did say them she discovered her 'hidden' thoughts and beliefs. This was her opportunity to rid herself of those and turn them round into positive affirmations. We also got her to concentrate on a positive affirmation to do with her weight. 'I am slim and gorgeous!' was the one that we chose between us instead of saying 'I don't want to be fat', (two negatives - 'don't' and 'fat'). Can you see that this new affirmation contained a positive present tense 'I am' and a positive 'slim and gorgeous'.

Over time she gradually began to become happy, healthy, contented and SLIM! Funnily enough, after a while, she didn't seem to need to be on a diet, although she did need some re-educating on what a healthy and nutritious diet was to start off with, including portion size and food combinations.

Case Study 2:

I hadn't seen my friend Debbie for a couple of months and was amazed to see that she was lovely and slim. I asked how she had managed it (I suspected she had not been on a diet as she is a holistic practitioner,) and she told me that she has practiced affirmations and gratitude at every meal and that was one of the ways she had lost it.

Her mantras were:

Thank you for this beautiful food.

May it provide me with optimum nourishment, health and vitality and help me achieve my natural healthy weight and perfect body.

Thank you to all the people who have provided this food for me and for humanity and may they appreciate their role in providing this food and may they always have ample food for themselves and their families.

Wow! Powerful stuff. She assured me that she changed nothing about her diet and actually ate very well. No cranky diet or starvation was required. She lost it mainly through the use of positive affirmations.

I am sure we can all think of a slim person who says 'I can eat what I want, I never put on weight' and a larger person who says 'I only have to *look* at a cream cake and I put on a pound!' – remember, be careful what you wish for, you might just get it! Remember Midas?

Increased Confidence

Positive affirmations have a knock-on effect beyond the result named in the affirmation. As your life gradually improves, you will feel a sense of growing confidence, whether or not you have ever phrased an affirmation regarding a boost in your confidence levels. This is the natural consequence of personal achievement. Your outlook on life changes and your self-image is transformed. You create a *virtuous circle* where a vicious one may have existed before.

Better Physical Health

As with confidence, an improvement in physical health will be a side-effect of positive affirmations, even when you have not phrased one that relates directly to your health. Negative emotions are draining on the psyche, and this can also have a debilitating effect on your physical well-being.

Negativity causes you to feel lethargic, and can cause genuine physical illness including depression, lethargy, infections and even cancer. Where positive affirmations can make you feel at ease, negative thoughts and habits cause you *dis*-ease. This is why people develop psychosomatic illnesses. The mind is a powerful thing. Imagine how wonderful it would be to feel healthy and full of vitality!

Psychosomatic means mind (psyche) and body (soma), and an illness of this sort therefore involves both the mind and the body. You will have heard the phrase 'sick with worry'. It is entirely possible to make yourself ill through stressful and negative thoughts. Some physical diseases are thought to be particularly affected by mental factors such as stress and anxiety. Psoriasis, eczema, stomach ulcers, IBS, high blood pressure, cancer and heart disease, for example, are all aggravated by negative thoughts. In fact, there is a mental aspect to how we react to, and cope with, physical disease.

Positive affirmations can improve your health in three ways: Firstly, your mindset is healthier overall with a positive mental attitude, thus your immune system is stronger; secondly, a specific affirmation can be phrased to augment your health and counter illness appearing; thirdly, they can be used to speed recovery if you do get ill.

David R Hamilton in 'How Your Mind Can Heal Your Body' explains how saying something over and over again creates neural connections in your brain. The more we say it the stronger the connections become.

Many people who are ill affirm their illness with words like 'I feel unwell', 'I will never get better', 'this is terrible', 'I feel tired'. And guess what they get?

If a sick person starts to change their attitude with more positive statement they can start to recover. Words like 'I am recovering', 'I am getting better', 'I feel much better today' or even 'Every day in every way, I am getting better and better.' These statements will start to create new neural pathways in the brain that will lead to recovery.

Both the *frequency* of affirmations and the *passion* that goes with them will speed up the process. If possible, make the affirmation 20 to 30 times a day, or every time the thought comes up for you. Do this for as long as it takes for the thing to manifest itself. You can't do this too often!

Happier Relationships

Positive affirmations create better relationships, as other people instinctively respond better to positive 'vibes' and success than to grumpiness and negativity. You are much more likely to have great relationships with others if you have a great relationship with yourself. Positive self-talk will aid with good relationships - if you do not like yourself then why would anyone else like you? People love to be with people who are happy, at peace, contented and giving.

This can affect every type of relationship in your life – with your partner, children, relatives, friends, acquaintances, strangers, work colleagues, and your boss.

Again, this is an area that will naturally improve as your affirmations take effect, even if they have not been targeted specifically at your relationships. You are far more likely to be successful if you have created a more attractive aura for yourself through positive affirmations.

Case study:

Jackie is my friend's mother and she is a very talented amateur artist but lacked confidence in her abilities. My friend and I visited one day and she got out all her mother's paintings to show me. I thought they were wonderful. But with every painting I was shown Jackie said 'Oh, that's not very good' or 'I don't really like that one'. I failed to find one that she liked! I was very positive about a couple of her paintings in particular and admired them for some time. Jackie just muttered about them not being very good. I pointed out that I thought they were good and I was enjoying looking at them. After a while I started getting tired of her negative comments and felt sorry that she was not justly proud of her work. I made my excuses and went home.

I later told my friend that I had struggled with meeting her mother and that I had found the experience very negative. I said that it was a shame her mother could not see her talent and success. I wanted her to feel good about her work and learn to take a compliment without throwing it back with negative comments each time.

My friend tactfully fed this back to her mother and gradually, with some more encouragement, her mother started to realise that her work is good, that other people do appreciate it, and that she should be happy to receive a complement about her work. As she grew in self confidence she appreciated her own work more and she was able to exhibit and sell her work and really enjoy creating her paintings too.

Susan Jeffers in her book 'Feel The Fear and Do It Anyway' describes how relationships can be enhanced by giving without expecting to get back, which is so much better than giving and expecting to be repaid. Expectations of others based on what you think they 'owe' you will always result in fear, resentment, disappointment and other negative emotions. When you really think about it you are programmed to expect something back and therefore probably experience disappointment on a regular basis.

If all your giving is about getting then think how fearful you become. If you fear not enough money, not enough love, not enough attention, or not enough praise, then you cannot genuinely give. If you seek approval, blame, or demand, then you are fearful. If you live your life constantly expecting, you will spend a great deal of your life disappointed that the world is not treating you right.

More will come back to us than we could ever imagine when we give, genuinely and with love, rather than from expectation. Genuine giving is not only altruistic but it makes *you* feel better too.

Start by giving away thanks – to those in your life now and those in your past. Thank them for their contribution to your life. Give away information, give away praise, give away compliments, give away time, give away money, give away love.

Lower your expectations and eventually give up expectation altogether and suddenly anything good that happens will be magnified and become fantastic! By not having expectations of others you will also be surprised at how much better relationships will become. All small acts of kindness and love are magnified and more noticeable than before. You will give good feedback and receive more in return!

Because Everything Begins in the Mind

> "He can if he thinks he can, he can't if he thinks he can't."
>
> Henry Ford

This statement by Henry Ford is the truth that underpins positive affirmations, and positive thinking generally. This is the concept that must be accepted if you are to truly embrace the possibility that positive affirmations can improve your life and bring success.

The easiest way to verify this statement is to simply look around you right now. Apart from Nature, everything you can see started life as a thought in the mind of a human being. The clothes you wear, the car you drive, the street you drive along, the house you live in, the TV you watch, the books you read, the computer you work at, the chair you sit on, the company you work for, *everything* started out as an idea in a mind of a person.

That should make you think. The power of your mind to invent and achieve is practically limitless. Everything that you are, or have achieved, began in your mind. Equally everything you are capable of doing also begins in your mind. You can start to design your dream life from this moment onwards!

"What the mind of man can conceive and believe, it can achieve."

Napoleon Hill in 'Think and Grow Rich'

Chapter 3
How To Make Affirmations

"Our imagination is the only limit to what we can hope to have in the future."
Charles Kettering

Let us now start to build your new *positive* life, the life of your *dreams*. Let us work on ridding yourself of negativity permanently!

Remember that affirmations program the mind, as you would program your computer. In the computing world there is an acronym: GIGO. It stands for: Garbage In, Garbage Out. This means that your computer can, and will, only respond to what is input into its system. If your machine is running cleanly, then you download and install a program and your computer crashes, it's likely that the program had a virus. If you put garbage into a computer, you can expect to get garbage out. This is the same for your mind, particularly your subconscious mind. And usually you don't even realize what has been put in!

1. Be Genuinely Positive

You cannot consistently program your mind with negativity and expect good things to be the result. When you approach the affirmations process, you must make certain that you do so with a positive frame of mind. Making successful affirmations is far more than speaking a few words in a set order. You may speak ten different affirmations each morning and evening, but if you don't really *believe* that the whole affirmation process can work, you will most likely follow each one with a negative thought or comment that messes up all your good work. For example:

You affirm: "I am a happy and successful person."

You think: *Yeah, right, in your dreams.*

You affirm: "I am a wealthy individual."

You think: *Maybe, once I win the lottery.*

You affirm: "My mind is at peace with the world."

You think: *When I'm half-cut perhaps.*

You get the idea. Making positive affirmations is not enough. You must believe them to be true to the exclusion of any and all counter-productive thoughts or feelings. Cynicism is a sure fire way to negate positive affirmations. This obviously needs some work, bad habits are hard to change. Apparently you have to do something

21 times to create or change a habit. So keep practicing! Remember to 'let go' any negative thoughts.

2. Use Positive Words

Although it may seem silly even mentioning that positive affirmations should be positive, this is an essential part of framing a positive affirmation and refers to the specific words you choose. For example, to quit smoking, you should not say: "I don't want to smoke any more." Instead, you could try: "I am free from smoking", or "I live a smoke-free, healthy life." Or "I am a non-smoker." Your affirmations should be about what you desire to happen, not about what you *don't* want to happen.

3. Use the Present Tense

We live our lives in the present moment. It may not seem that way when you are worrying about the future or regretting the past, but there is really nothing more than what is happening *now*. We hear people say that you have to live in the moment, and we understand the sense in doing so, but it remains notoriously difficult to truly master.

However, in positive thinking, and in positive affirmations especially, the present tense is paramount; try to hone your ability to actually live in the moment, certainly develop your willingness to accept its importance in reprogramming your mind.

Your mind works in the present tense. It knows no other way to think. We create a past for ourselves in our memories and the emotions attached to them. We build a future for ourselves with our hopes, goals, dreams and desires, or fears and sorrows. But our *mind* lives in the *now*. This means that any negative thoughts about your past that you carry with you at this moment *create your present*. You are perpetuating your past.

You know how this works. If you recall a very sad event, even from many years ago, it can probably still make you cry. Your mind is interpreting this memory as happening now, and creates an appropriate response. It cannot differentiate between what happened ten years ago and what happened ten seconds ago; it can only react to what is in your mind right now. It also cannot distinguish between reality and imagination! Now there's a thought.

The upshot for your positive affirmations is that they must be phrased so that the mind can act upon them at this moment in time, therefore you *must* use the present tense. Once you begin to realise this it provides you with a powerful tool to make a difference to your thoughts.

Let's take an obvious example, and assume you want to be rich. You have three options as to how this is phrased:

➢ The past tense – In this case you might say: "I always wanted to be rich." Your mind takes this to mean that you did want to be rich but not any more, therefore it does not take the required actions to bring it about.

➢ The future tense – In this case, you might say: "I will be a rich person." This might seem the obvious choice because you are planning for your future, but this is also the wrong way to phrase your affirmations. Your mind interprets this as meaning that you will be rich in the future, but not now, so fails to take any action.

➢ The present tense – In this scenario, you might say: "I am a rich person." Don't worry, your mind is not going to take issue with you on this because you may not actually have very much money (although it may come up with some negative self-talk initially); rather it will respond by attempting to create the circumstances to match the affirmation. You have, in effect, given your mind an order that must be acted upon *now*.

If this smacks a little of self-delusion, this is just something you will have to deal with for now. You are programming your mind in the way it must be programmed to work powerfully for you.

Clearly, you have to exercise a little caution here. Telling your mind you are rich does not instantly put money in the bank. If you see a Ferrari drive by, you can say: "That Ferrari is my car", but that does not mean you should run to your bank and withdraw all your savings to put down a deposit at your local Ferrari dealership. Such behaviour will obviously provoke immense panic on your part especially if you realize you can't even buy a tin of beans for dinner! And thus it will work against your positive attitude.

Talking in the present tense is not about deluding yourself or ignoring your current reality; *it is about giving your mind orders in the language it best understands.*

4. Be Passionate

This almost goes without saying, because if you have heartfelt desires you should automatically be passionate about them. However, there may be times in your life when the burdens of the world are weighing on you and your affirmations take a knock. Your mood drops and you cannot summon the enthusiasm for even those people or things closest to your heart. Just remember that this can become a vicious circle, and the only way to break it is to replace your negativity with positive thoughts. Making the effort to repeat your affirmations passionately can help resurrect your mood in a very short time, or even instantly. It may help to remember a time when you felt passionate about something and how that felt at the time, then capture that feeling for your affirmations now.

5. Add Visualization and Other Senses

This may come naturally to some people who think in visual images, but it is something everyone should be practicing when they speak their positive affirmations. This is most effective when you have a little quiet time for your affirmations, so you can sit down and close your eyes and back up your words with your senses.

Let's stick with the Ferrari example. Owning a Ferrari might represent the pinnacle of achievement for some people. It may be the only affirmation they utter, because they know that they will only come to own one through the attainment of riches generally.

So here's the affirmation: "I own a red Ferrari F430 Spider." Naming the car, and even the colour, makes it specific and personal and allows for a deeper emotional involvement. But to make this affirmation as powerful as possible, you should know what one looks like so you can visualize it in your mind and see yourself sitting in it; you should know what one sounds like; you should be able to smell the leather interior; you should be able to feel the vibrations from the engine.

Your intention must be to convince your mind that your affirmation is real in every detail, and this means bringing as many senses into play as possible. You can do this in a number of ways. Start by finding a picture of the car. Put the picture up in a prominent place and repeat your affirmation. Close your eyes and imagine getting into it, starting the engine, the sound it makes, putting it into gear and driving off – FAST! Have fun with it! Create your own 'home movie' of you driving and enjoying the car. Keep repeating so the image becomes more and more clear.

6. Be Patient and Persevere

There is a saying: "Good things come to those who wait." Affirmations do not always produce immediate results, so be prepared for this. Unless you win the lottery, your dreams of instant riches may be unrealistic. Depending on the desired outcome of your affirmation, you may be waiting days, weeks, months or years. Be patient and keep up with your affirmations. But *know* that they will happen.

By having your mind open to your dreams you will start to see opportunities to fulfil them.

7. As Often as Possible

Your affirmations need to be spoken regularly for them to be effective. This is where the analogy with computers ends. You program a computer once and it is all set up. Not so with affirmations. Affirmations work with repetition. In this respect, it is more akin to training a puppy. You get it to obey the command to sit, but the next time it is too interested in chewing your shoe. It is only with repetition that the penny finally drops and you achieve your desired results. The mind needs to be trained in exactly the same manner.

Your mind is prone to drifting and going its own sweet way. It is used to falling back into negative self-talk. This is why so many people are at the mercy of their emotions and their thoughts; why their lives seem so out of control.

The orders you give to your mind need to be given regularly. Could you train a dog by telling it to "Sit!" once a week? Equally, no matter how many times you told it, could you train a dog by telling it "I always wanted you to sit!", or "You will sit tomorrow!"? The only way to do it is to speak in the present tense and repeat the order until the message gets through. This also highlights the importance of keeping your affirmations short and to the point. This makes them easier to remember and punchier.

As for exactly how many times to repeat your affirmations, the answer is *as often as possible*. You should always strive to do this in the morning and the evening out loud. These might be 5 to 10 minute sessions that really focus the mind. However, the time in the morning when you are still half-asleep in bed is also ideal because your brainwaves are still in 'alpha', which is considered the optimum brainwave activity for connection with your inner mind.

During the day, of course there will be times when you are concentrating on other matters, but there will also be numerous opportunities when it is possible to repeat your affirmations. Whenever your mind is free, put it to work on your affirmations. Even if you cannot speak out loud or close your eyes and engage your senses, you can still repeat your affirmations mentally to yourself.

As far as possible, try to attain a relaxed mood during your affirmations. Stress and tension detract from your mind's ability to focus.

I love this affirmation, described as The Perfect Affirmation from the book 'The Secret' by Rhonda Byrne:

> *"I am whole, perfect, strong, loving, harmonious and happy."*
>
> Charles Harnell

Chapter 4
Useful Affirmations

"Remember, no more effort is required to aim high in life, to demand abundance and prosperity, than is required to accept misery and poverty"
Napoleon Hill

Here are a few ideas for affirmations. More are given in Chapter 7 on page 55).

For Love and Peace
- I am happy
- My mind is at peace
- I am calm and relaxed at all times
- My thoughts are under my control
- I am surrounded by love
- I radiate love and peace
- I have a loving relationship with my wife/husband/partner
- I am at peace with the Universe
- I love and accept myself
- I am surrounded by loving people
- I am loving and accepting of others

- I trust the wisdom of my inner being
- I am always connected with Divine Love

For Prosperity and Success

- I am getting wealthier every day
- I study and learn fast
- I have the perfect job/business
- I am living in my dream house
- I am successful in whatever I do
- I always have enough money
- I am successful in everything I do
- I am loving the progress I am making every day
- Everything is getting better every day

For Health
- My body is healthy and strong
- I have lots of energy and vitality
- The food I eat nourishes me

- I am becoming fitter and healthier each day

- I feel younger and more energetic every day

- I maintain my ideal weight

Obviously, you can tinker with these and come up with your own to exactly suit your personal goals and desires. Just remember to keep them positive, present tense, and passionate.

Declarations

Sometimes it is useful to make a *declaration*. The difference is subtle but definite. A declaration is where you declare out loud, preferably in front of as many people as possible, something that you intend to do. For example "I am going to retire when I am 55" or "I am going to climb Mount Everest!"

A declaration tends to be made once. If it is made in front of others then it is much more powerful, because the audience will hold you accountable – they heard you say it after all! By making it in front of others you are also asking for support to make it happen. If people, particularly those close to you, know your intentions then they can help you make them come true (hopefully!).

Making declarations should be only done if you are serious about what you are saying or you will lose credibility with others, and even yourself.

Declarations shouldn't be made too often either or they lose their punch.

You can also make private declarations. This is ideally done in front of a mirror whilst you look yourself in the eye. To add some gravity, to public and private declarations, put your hand on your heart and make sure you say it with feeling too.

Chapter 5
Cosmic Affirmations

"Strange and marvelous things will happen with constant regularity as we alter our lives and begin to live in harmony with the Laws of the Universe."
Earl Nightingale

You should now understand very well how affirmations can be used to improve the quality of your thoughts at a personal, internal, level. It is not difficult to grasp how a positive attitude can create a more attractive and amenable personality, so that other people respond more positively in return. Your internal dialogue will dictate who you are and how you feel. And this is now under your control (with practice).

However, there is another aspect to affirmations that we have not yet covered, and that is how positive thoughts are transmitted to the Universe, to the outside of you. This is an area that requires a leap of faith, although there is also sound evidence for believing that such a form of communication is possible.

Firstly, let's look at what this deals with. The implication here is that we are a minuscule part of a cosmic whole. That cosmic whole is the creator of everything in the universe and it goes by various names. Some obviously refer to it as God or the Divine; others who are not religious call it the Universal Mind, Universal Consciousness, or Cosmic Power. As we are a part of it, so our thoughts are connected with it, and we can therefore communicate our thoughts and desires to it. As it is the ultimate creator of everything in existence, and continues to be so, it is thus able to reply to our desires and create the exact circumstances in our lives that we have requested. However, just like our own minds, the Universal Mind is an order-taker and so we have to be extremely careful what we ask for, i.e. what you *think of* or *say* in your affirmations.

It is not unusual for people to balk at this idea. We look in the mirror and see a separate entity, connected to nothing else around us in physical terms other than the ground we stand on. Our border is defined by our skin, and it is therefore easy to doubt a connection to anything outside ourselves. However, your mobile phone is also a separate entity, yet you do not deny its ability to connect you with another person on the other side of the world with no wires involved. Why then is it such a leap to suppose there is a form of communication that might allow our thoughts to be sent half way around the world, and to all parts of the world?

There is certainly plenty of anecdotal evidence of telepathic abilities in humans, and many laboratory tests have proven that information can be transmitted from one person's mind to another in a remote location. Perhaps this is the tip of the iceberg. Perhaps these people are just the select few who are aware of their abilities. It might be that we all have this power but are not sufficiently aware of it to bother trying to channel it.

Thankfully, to a certain extent, science can help us overcome our doubts about universal communication. In scientific terms, everything in the universe is made up of just one thing: atoms. The atom is a basic unit of matter consisting of a central nucleus surrounded by a cloud of negatively-charged electrons. Although this matter may take on different forms – solid, liquid, gas and plasma – we see different objects all around us, *everything* is matter.

More importantly, the atoms in your body are actually 99.99% vacuum, they are pure energy. These are the same atoms that are found in everything else in the universe. Energy is in us, flows through us, and is all around us. We may not be able to see it, but we are all connected to each other and to everything else in the universe.

Think of the air you are breathing. It is inside you and all around you, and inside every other living thing as well. We are all connected.

Although it is certainly not proof beyond a reasonable doubt, it does at least provide a theoretical reason why your affirmations can be carried far and wide.

Law of Attraction

The Law of Attraction is one of the Universal Laws. These are also referred to as Spiritual Laws or Laws of Nature. Universal Laws are those immutable principles that rule our world and our universe, governing how the entire cosmos continues to exist and thrive.

Universal Laws work whether we believe in them or not. Those who do not believe in them choose, by default, to believe that life is a random series of events that they have little or no control over, and that there is no purpose or underlying reason why things happen as they do.

The Law of Attraction gives you what you are thinking about. It is like a magnet, it draws things to you through your thoughts. The problem is most people can only think about what they *don't* want. If you want wealth for instance then you need to be thinking about wealth and abundance, not lack, limitation and debt.

One of the common sayings in positive thinking is: "Whatever the mind of man can conceive of, and believe in, it can achieve."

Affirmations tap into the Law of Attraction – they help you to manifest what you desire. Your affirmations are also a way of putting out a 'request' to the Universe, to let it know what you desire. What you think about will come about –

whether it is good or bad. You can 'attract' bad health, poor relationships, or poverty as easily as you can attract wealth, great relationships and health and vitality. By using affirmations and tapping into the Law of Attraction circumstances and events will soon start to work towards your desires. You may meet a person who can give you a piece of information that you need, you will start to see opportunities that didn't seem to be there before. You will be amazed at how powerful this is!

For more information about the Law of Attraction read Rhonda Byrne's book *The Secret*.
(also available as a video and audio book for visual and auditory learners)

Chapter 6
The Chemistry of Affirmations

"To enjoy good health, to bring true happiness to one's family, to bring peace to all, one must first discipline and control one's own mind. If a man can control his mind he can find the way to Enlightenment, and all wisdom and virtue will naturally come to him."
The Buddha

Before you can hope to master the Universe, however, you must learn to master yourself, and so we will end with a return to the more personal level, and a popular theory from internationally-respected neuroscientist, Dr Candace Pert, Ph.D. Her theories, based on her discovery of opiate receptors – cellular binding sites for brain endorphins – and her further laboratory research, may explain exactly how your thoughts and affirmations create your personal reality.

What follows provides a completely different perspective on why we must watch our thoughts at all times and try to maintain a healthy, positive mental attitude.

This first part is fact. Human beings are made up of around 50 trillion eukaryote cells, which are cells with a nucleus that carries our DNA. The fact that each of these does carry DNA means that each one contains the equivalent of all the body's functional systems – nervous, circulatory, digestive, respiratory, excretory, endocrine, immune, muscle and skeletal, skin and reproductive. Each cell is a living organism in its own right, and has the capability to grow as a single entity when placed in a Petri dish. Consider the furore over stem-cell research at the moment because of its potential to essentially create human body parts.

Now to the crucial issue that impacts your affirmations – the theory of how these cell receptors may be responsible for your emotional make-up.

Pert, through her research, believes that your emotions are triggered by a part of the brain called the hypothalamus, which is known to be responsible for certain metabolic processes and other activities of the Autonomic Nervous System. She believes that when your thoughts provoke an emotion, your hypothalamus creates a chemical that is matched to that particular emotion. These chemicals are called peptides, or neuropeptides, which are sequences of small chain amino acids – the building blocks of protein.

Each time you have a certain emotional thought, the hypothalamus releases the same related chemical into the bloodstream. It travels through your body and seeks out cells, each of which can have over 1000 receptor sites, some of which will be receptors for that particular peptide. When the peptide locks onto these sites, the proteins in the peptide are released into the cells and physically change their structure. The cells then create the given emotion throughout the body.

The more often a certain emotion is felt, the quicker the receptor sites are found on the cells and the quicker the emotion is experienced, and the deeper it is felt. This would clearly have catastrophic consequences if the emotions we feel most of the time are negative. This may be why depression can take hold so quickly and be so hard to lift out of.

But remember where this all starts as a *thought* in our mind.

Here's the theory simplified:

- You have an emotional thought
- Your hypothalamus releases an appropriate peptide
- That peptide enters the bloodstream
- It locks onto cell receptor sites
- It enters the cell and alters its structure

- We feel the emotion

So you can see that thoughts produce feelings and these have the potential to affect every cell in your body.

However, the power of positive affirmations does not stand or fall on the ultimate proving or disproving of any theory. No matter what causes affirmations to work, they *do* work.

Always remember: *Your thoughts can change your life.* Positive affirmations have the power to bring about the circumstances in your life that will allow you to become the successful person you always desired to be. To live the life of your dreams!

> "Good thoughts and actions can produce bad results; bad thoughts and actions can never produce good results."
>
> James Allen

Chapter 7
Affirmations for everyday use

"If you can dream it you can do it."

Walt Disney

Here are some more examples of affirmations that you might find useful for everyday situations. You can obviously create your own once you get the hang of them and start to see the results. Print them on a small card, laminate them and keep them in your pocket or purse.

Another tip is to record your affirmations onto a portable recording machine and listen to yourself saying them. Leave enough space between affirmations to allow time for you to repeat them out loud. If you can, add some stirring music, that also helps.

10 Golden Rules of good affirmations

1. Always say them in the present tense – for example "I am …", "I have…", "I do …", "I always …".

2. Always make them positive and focusing on what you WANT not what

you don't want – for example – "I am slim and healthy and full of energy". Saying "I don't want to be fat" or "I don't smoke" are double negatives and will not work!

3. Say them out loud and with enthusiasm and passion, several times each day, when in a relaxed state. Try saying them to yourself whilst looking in the mirror.

4. Make them realistic and achievable but at the same time don't dumb them down – think big and expand your dreams! Maybe choose some more realistic ones to start with to prove to yourself that it works and after a few weeks expand them to something much bigger.

5. Write them down and keep them with you. You can then make sure you are always saying them correctly and you can say them whenever you have a few moments.

6. Be careful what you wish for – remember Midas who wished for everything he touched to turn to gold? That included his wife and child! Where possible choose affirmations that will help you work towards the greater good.

7. Persevere! Don't give up because nothing seems to be happening.

8. Review your affirmations every month or

so to ensure they are still serving you.

9. Add visualization to your affirmation – imagine yourself doing that thing or having that thing or create a picture to go with it.
10. Record your own to make them personal.

Feel free to use the following affirmations to get you started. These are divided up into subject areas that you might wish to concentrate on.

- Empowering Affirmations
- Affirmations for good relationships
- Affirmations for happiness
- Affirmations for a fulfilling life
- Affirmations for work and career

Empowering Affirmations

I love my life

I am happy

I am healthy and full of energy

I am whole, perfect and strong

I am loving, harmonious and happy

Everything is going according to plan

I am living my dreams

I am excited about my present and my future

I have plans that motivate me

I have written goals and review them regularly

I take action every day to constantly move towards my dreams

I go with confidence

I am worthy of everything I do and everything I plan to do

Everything I do is effortless and happening perfectly

I accept this moment as it is

This moment is as it should be

I know that problems hold the seeds of opportunity

I have choice and I always make good choices that bring me fulfillment and happiness

I make good decisions that benefit me and others

I ask my heart for guidance

I know I am capable of anything I choose to do

I am in harmony with nature

I am part of the universe and open to all its power, energy and information

I let the universe know what I want, and leave the details to the universe

I know it will provide

I love my life

I am living my dreams

Affirmations for good relationships

I love myself

I am loved and love others

I am on good terms with everyone

I make other people happy

I have fulfilling relationships with my loved ones and people I know

I accept things as they are

I accept people, situations, events and circumstances as they happen

This moment is as it should be

I forgive others and seek forgiveness

I show interest in others

I always treat others with respect

I am happy and grateful for my family

I am happy and grateful for my friends

I am happy and grateful for those I love

I care deeply about others

I wish others peace, joy and laughter

I accept love and compliments from others

I am open to all points of view

I let others tell their story

I am flexible and have no need to defend my point of view

I never condemn

I give to others compliments, praise and love

I give appreciation

I remember people's names

I only talk about someone as if they are in the room with me

Wherever and whenever I can, I help others to be happy and fulfilled

I keep my desires to myself

I love life

I am happy

I love to smile and make others smile

I love to laugh and make others laugh

I am confident

I go with grace

I am at peace

Affirmations for happiness

I love life

I am happy

Everything is happening perfectly and with ease

Everything is going according to plan

I accept this moment as it is

This moment is as it should be

I enjoy making plans and seeing them come to pass

I know what I want and know I will get there

I have choice and always make good choices that bring me fulfillment and happiness

I ask my heart for guidance

I pay attention to those things I wish to improve

I go with intention to improve my life and the lives of others

I am happy and aim to make others happy

I wish others peace, joy and laughter

I smile often and make others smile

I laugh often and make others laugh

I have fulfilling relationships with others

I live in grace

I am at peace

I am grateful for my wonderful life and for the gift of life

I am grateful I am healthy

I am grateful I am happy

I am grateful I am wealthy

I am grateful I am loved

I am happy and fulfilled

Affirmations for a fulfilling life

I love life

I am happy

I am powerful

I am loved and love others

I am whole, perfect, strong, loving, harmonious and happy

I am confident and certain of my ability to achieve what I choose

I know I am capable of anything I wish to achieve

I am so happy and grateful that I am successful

I mix with those people who are better than me and will teach me how to achieve more in my life

I have more than enough money for my needs and to help others

I am so happy and grateful that money comes to me in increasing quantities, on a continuous basis, from multiple sources

I am totally responsible for my life

I am totally responsible for my feelings

I am totally responsible for my results.

I am successful

I am excited about my present and my future

I have energy and enthusiasm to improve my life and the lives of others

Everything I do is effortless and happening perfectly

I am in harmony with nature

I care deeply about the world

I receive the gifts of nature such as the warming sun, the refreshing rain and the air I breathe

I am part of the universe and open to its power, energy and information

I let the universe know what I want and leave the details to the universe

I know it will provide

I am living my dreams

I am a happy, healthy, confident person!

Affirmations for work and career

I am on good terms with all people

I go with confidence and grace

I smile and make others smile

I enjoy working with others and they enjoy working with me

I care deeply about others

I respect others and see their point of view

I show appreciation of others

I show interest in others

I give praise

I am fair and just and expect that of others

I take responsibility for my current situation

I celebrate my successes and help others celebrate their successes

I keep my desires to myself

I have the energy and enthusiasm to move forward in my career and to help others move forward too

My career goals are happening as planned

Everything I do is effortless and happening perfectly

I make good decisions that benefit me and others

I have choice and always make good choices that bring me fulfillment and happiness

I am rewarded well for my efforts

I am worthy of my rewards

I enjoy the benefits of my rewards

I enjoy my rest and my holidays

I love my work and constantly strive to improve

I have valuable skills and constantly build on them to improve myself

I help others to enjoy their work and feel fulfilled

I see problems as seeds of opportunity

I strive to find the answers to challenges

I am creative

I find ways to work more efficiently and effectively

I am not alone

I know that if I wish to leave this job I will immediately find a better one

I am so happy and grateful for my career

I am so happy and grateful that my career fulfils me and helps others

I am so happy and grateful that I enjoy my work and working with others

I love my work

And Finally…

I hope that you have now started to understand the power of affirmations to alter your mindset and empower you to reach whatever it is you desire. You now need to try them out and see how powerful they are. Be patient, be persistent and enjoy noticing the difference it makes to your life.

Enjoy!

Peace and Love

Sue

One today is worth two tomorrows; never leave that till tomorrow which you can do today.
Benjamin Franklin

Further Reading

The Secret by Rhonda Byrne

Feel the Fear and Do It Anyway by Susan Jeffers

You Can Heal Your Life by Louise L Hay

How Your Mind Can Heal Your Body by David R Hamilton

Destiny is not a matter of chance; it is a matter of choice. It is not a thing to be waited for; it is a thing to be achieved.

William Jennings Bryan

For my children, Rebecca and David, whom I love dearly.